HYPERBOREAL

PITT POETRY SERIES
ED OCHESTER, EDITOR

HYPERBOREAL

JOAN NAVIYUK KANE

UNIVERSITY OF PITTSBURGH PRESS

Published by the University of Pittsburgh Press, Pittsburgh, Pa., 15260
Manufactured in the United States of America
Printed on acid-free paper
10 9 8 7 6 5 4 3 2 1

ISBN 13: 978-0-8229-6262-5
ISBN 10: 0-8229-6262-4

This book is the winner of the 2012 Donald Hall Prize in Poetry, awarded by
the Association of Writers and Writing Programs (AWP). AWP, a national
organization serving more than three hundred colleges and universities, has its
headquarters at George Mason University, Mail Stop 1E3, Fairfax, VA 22030.

The Donald Hall Prize for Poetry is made possible by the generous support of
Amazon.com.

for my children, aluuram pigiyaa

CONTENTS

HYPERBOREAL

I.

Hyperboreal

Arnica nods heavy-headed on the bruised slope.
Peaks recede in all directions, in heat-haze,
Evening in my recollection.

The shield at my throat ornamental and worse.
We descended the gully thrummed into confusion
With the last snowmelt a tricklet into mud, ulterior —

One wolfbane bloom, iodine-hued, rising on its stalk
Into the luster of air: June really isn't June anymore,
Is it? A glacier's heart of milk loosed from a thousand

Summer days in extravagant succession,
From the back of my tongue, dexterous and sinister.

At Anaktuvuk Pass

Motherless on the cusp of the Giant's Valley
I am childless, reduced.

Stark things bellow all about me,
Dusted with new snow and inaccessible.

The pass runnels off its axis, lapsing
A few degrees from true north: devoid,

Our dialect differs. *Miluk* a mountain's name.
Barren-ground caribou arriving beneath it

From *Napakrualuit*, a place that looks like trees.
Once anointed with grease and ashes—

Now distant from sage, sorrel, and stinging nettle,
Divided into self again.

In a House Apart

You hurt me, then,
Burnt a bird's white plumage—
Claim that we are the better for it,
That we will heal in time.

Strident and inaccurate
Despite all proximity,
The mountains no longer
Made me feel better.

The year in its wheel of winter
And its small cylinder of light
In excess. Far pillars could
Resemble human figures

Though only rock rises
From some progression
Of dust, demand, and rotten
Wood. I place my hand on stone

And become stone myself.

Akkumin Qanituq/Swift Descent

for Paniqrak Quyuraq

Words turn to dry grass
               beneath my cramped foot,
Anger to grease ice
               on the sea, once turbulent.

In another room I hear her voice over
Again the creaking of the pipes.

In another room she has not gone
Unforgiven and shunned.

Another room is filled with light,
As full as her white wall tent
The summer that she took me in,

Pressed fresh leaves against my wounds
As if
               as if to heal them.

Disappearer

*Disappearance, extinction, the inability to survive as a race—these
are the anxieties of an Inuit modernity. They lie at the fuzzy border
between cultural and biological extinction.*
   —Lisa Stevenson

*Issriliuġnailat naniq atausiq kuguumazina.man. Taavrumuŋa ipkua
Ugiuvaŋmiut taimana itpazuktut. / They did not get cold as long as
just a single oil lamp was burning. For that reason, the King Islanders
were able to survive.*
   —Pikkuŋana / Aloysius Pikonganna

in a city of seven too many corners

uncle struck and left to die
in rain torrential
in the road in the dark

adrift without relations

sister twenty at suicide
having left her son swaddled
in the clothes of my own

a black snow fell

aunt whose court-appointed custodian
spent the money meant for heat
on beer and snuff and spirits

unable to grasp the trailing dragline

grandfather with a cerebral aneurysm
deposited at jail instead of hospital
the police mistaking him for drunk

we hear constant surf

cousin skids off the road
what's left of a six-pack
locked rolling in her trunk

for the sea is very deep

land's end *nunam izua*

let us set the last stone in place

Fugato (1)

Nail in her mouth in a stone-girded house held fast by cords,
Now I don't know anymore. Nail on a stone-strewn shore
Where the river widens into the sea. To a large rock
I fasten her mittens, which at dusk transforms—

I will walk back myself. Line of horizon
Drawn into focus with ocher and fat,

With the tide it swims away.

Mysteries of Light

Loosen the ropes.
Seven lances in her heart put forth blossoms.

Beneath a torrent, refuge—
As a little child with a medallion of chased gold

Aboard a ship, with birds
About her shoulder and a magpie on her hand.

An axe lodged in the roof,
A wolf whose mouth will proclaim.

One breast on a plate. Stone in hand.
Red egg, wool, sometimes a wound in her forehead.

Called to the ditches alongside the mine roads,
A continuation of things we do wrong.

II.

Love Poem

If there was rain,
It was incessant.

If there was wind,
I walked into it.

If there were stars,
Suddenly they were more
Typic, ever brighter
In a sky that was trouble

Until you skirred past
Under it, somehow drawing
Near on the sheet of ice
Between us.

You do not know
How little I loved
Before I loved you.

Spared the hell variant,
Spoor a metaphor.
The ulu skidding
Over the brittle
Surface of the river,
Returning it to water.

A motif of pursuit
In the bones
Of an eagle.

I was the girl
Who refused to marry.

In the totality of sleep
We dream together.

Gorge

What I cannot suppose
As part of another life—

No bone to give hot broth,
No game between walls.

We beg a precipice,
A great gulf.

A small practitioner of earth,
I am learned from this—

This a stray, a hunt riot,
The custody of a wilderness.

Muġŋatuŋilana/I am not tired

I was beneath linked stars
One among many exiles—

The returned light floods
Again a world unmoved,

Its translucent sky rifts
At a ring of mountains.

I could cup the small stone
Of the heart percussing.

Moving in the muddy arc
Of a thing afloat as pebbles

Slope toward the shores' end,
Turning toward them warm

And familiar. The ocean, eared,
Roaring and familiar.

Intervale

The sun
    made new again
Shadows of ice

As vertebra
    cut through.

A plain of grit,
    a sediment.

From
    the forest
The wind
    had all revised,

A nest thrown
    into our path

Intact: moose hair
    and moss.

With their blue
    and distant taper,

We hold in poise
    mountains: stone on

Stone upon stone.

Drawn Together

Shot through with white, error—
A dream of birds of prey returned
Dropping glyptics, baskets.

Last night's lopped moon
Couldn't put into words
The ink around it.

Split and cleft,
I no longer weaken into sleep.
I no longer ash,

Ache. No carrion bird
Blown into the city,
No house on fire, no.

The Dissolve of Voices

There are seven moons tonight,
                              and somehow boughs
beyond the scaffolds. In the streets she was lost to me.

In the streets I have imagined light, a kind of it,
though it too has long since vanished—

It cannot be summoned through fire or smoke
or other oblivions as all the men fall away like snow,
settling into new designs of havoc
                              until sifted
anew in gusts, in passing. After all, I look down
and do believe evasion is not a home.

In the wing bones, a susurration. A squirrel
          snare for our relations. A reason
for the patterns of our movements, dances:

A truss of staffs bound with bands stained by alder.

The rivers glossal. A mask subsumed in a mass
of stones that seem something like a man.

Bladder
          blood
                    and lung
     of a bear dropped from exhaustion.

A love absolute of places unknown to me:

aġnaġuksram izrizrvia, ipkanaqtuat, aniraaq,
miziktaagvik, uavat, kassanait, qiniġa.wik.

In a warm room we were altered, alter
together: beyond this, comprehended for a plural.

Fugato (2)

Another light, another answer—
Pith of the moon visible through low clouds.
Worry treads gray circles somewhere else.

Thinking he is lost,
He shall remember that this is the sky
With everything in it.

Etch

Wavelessly, against
Flatland: the ocean,

The sun, hanging.

He carved the light, though
The world remains

Unmoved. Wind furls

Sashes of dry snow
Across the road,

Hoar nacres electrical
Transformers. I was

Cochlear, curving, bone

Handed me the eardrum
Of a bowhead whale—

Veined and furrowed.

Listening, I began
To know so little.

The Fire

Nothing dry accumulates.
An assay of a blown glass
Bird, the unfastened

Patterns of fluted beads,
Silt and sand, or
Something fractured.

Talc, panes scattered,
A heavy vial, and then whole
Clear pharmacies, jars

And bottles. It does choose
What it does not break.

III.

Ivory, Stomach, Bone

This is what I expected:
Those who make a small fire,
A flame agitated by wind.

Those two among you
Who will never
      name one another
Will not survive.

Stepping backward
At the meeting of rivers
I lose time.

The wind gusts
Her white hair away
      up through rough
Shore ice.

Out of the black border
He lugs a stump
Of driftwood & four boughs

Oh woman,
      lapidated woman,
What would it have taken
To see your heart?

Mother Tongues

Through a tangle of alder
I could make passage
A thousand obscure,
Contradictory ways.

Some ruin
Of a renounced thing.
Some measure
For retraction in its red

Declension. By fix
Of milk in saltwater,
Blood in milk. Our
Division of phrase

From fact. Mother,
Aakaa; Woman,
Aġnaq. Already
In naming my sons,

You foresee the last time
We will be able to talk
Together—I, daughterless,
And you, who knew.

Force Majeur

      in unusual fuse
our storms arise suddenly,
walrus and bear resolve
to each other.

Masterful in one element,
while in another
      a boot fills with piss.

Always snow, the path no easier—
now in shadow
      with katabatic winds
downing boughs of spruce and birch.

Though together we are born and live,
one must finish another.

On Either Side

At the rim of the world, the aching world,
a fault of snow and shadow.
She predicts sense yet I find none:
nothing, in fact, but the edges of things,
in wind and the movement of animals.

Through dreams inlaid with rigid marrow
at last I grew to grasp her fear:
it was to have been a survivor
when there were no others.
Between my dreams, the net of them,

light breaks above an oyster midden
as one day yokes itself to another.
She could not be farther—
somewhere near the mingled voices
of boys as they gather rocks for slingshots.

Hers a force as vital as my own disgrace:
the pulse of it plays back at me.
There is no final story,
no assertion, no deception.
I may never know who I am.

I splint the stem broken in recurrence
from leaning so many times,
and smother the roots in sand.
The shoot shifts ever toward the light.

For the Man with Sealfinger

With its line of distant junction,
Rain stops the air.
A white sound, unison.

Of a long arc, cranes
Aggregate and stage. Soon
To kneel by brackish water,

Watch them circle,
Gain altitude, and
Move directly eastward.

Setting calls to settle
In the heartrot of birches:
I, too, would listen.

Time and Time Again

in the days before your birth
your heart beat out some worry

in our two rooms above two tiŋmiaġruat
perpetually atop the rooftop opposite

those ravens unstilled a strange cluster
of birches' black dendritic branches

in my narrow recollection
we lost sight of land altogether

through failure to keep the shore
we labored across the open water

kept to method of nothing
but counting stars

perhaps my fingers I allowed
to drop into the sea

her vaticination of a child
to be born without hands

a lapse as she also thought me
made of wood

when the light returns
it will be something like a spring

the source of a stream
the slit cave at the breast

of the island
oh to rip apart the world

Craft

Does not require shavings
Of wood, tusk-dust furrowed
By drill, the embossment of beads
Or skin-sole crimped between teeth—

As in a plane sped to spot
The birds beneath, when
Something seems to say
Here, every trace of us ends.

What construction to lend me
In the moment when I would not
Recall the song I was to sing?

It will catch in the rickrack
Of my garment, the porcupine
Quill in the left of my ear.

In Long Light

The sooty night a backdrop
for a slip of rowan trees,
swans in migration.
Beneath the ice
in its interminable thaw
streams improbable
but assuredly there—
these things contained,
not trapped by the world.
What I mean to say is,
I am not sure I will ever
become the person
I had hoped, or forgive
myself the inaccuracy
of estimation. It is
one thing to blame
the glare of the sun
and another to be held
(but not bound) through the
long fermata of dusk
and its promised repetition.

Looking Through

I.

I follow a new life,
Along with you
And the sea

Which never seems to move—
Teaching the children
How not to fear the ocean,

To leave me, go away,
And not come back.

II.

Mud flats   history opaque
And without new variant.

Near freezing, the water is nothing
To be dissolved into and the light

Never gives me a reason to do anything.
Instead, we walk together uphill,

Only to speak of something beautiful
About invisible technique, proportion

In a circle of fish:
Another blue abstraction.

III.

I make you a stranger. Here,
There are too many angles.
The hills of home always in contour,
Their trees turning from the top down.

Between us is the matter at hand,
Something different from its sources.

Games of Strength

Staggering cold, consigned to oblivion
And unafraid to see again—
A barrier of white a protection from harm.

Each blue line a vein swelling with blood
Until the swift death of asphalt, fracture.
Our low art a burden of memory.

Through wakefulness sublux, sural and dull,
I retrieve those beads of tooth, bone and brown,
Meant as a circlet for my wrist.

Field Notes

The bitter yield of the waste bed
a bucketful of dandelion wine.
A raven's slit tongue. God's eye,
           the wound that opens.

Motionless *Aegolius funereus*—
An omen: typical, resplendent.

Her medicament stripped from the yew tree.

Ensnared, they did not allow X to fall
Which of course is the cause of such trouble.

Ash, resin, and ruin. All loves
Not love but adhesion,
           and anywhere but here.

Fugato (3)

Catching the crook of a bone
On the point of a needle,

Her hand declares her all too human.

Procession

I.

Several arrows embedded her chest,
But she did not die.

It is said that she had her eyes closed,
But she did not die.

She got up from where she slept;
How long she slept she did not know,

But she did not die.

II.

These days—
Even here on the mainland,

The sun drops down lower in the sky.
The dog is unchained.

The window is broken.
The swans have flown away—

III.

Turn the light on,
It is time for church,
And then I will go to a meeting.

They were very strong,
Our ancestors of long ago.
They do not see us.

Maliktuk

I.

Marraa qaġrut pulaarut qatigaakiŋun,
Tuġusuilaq.

Siguġniŋaruġuuq tavra.
Tuġusuilaq.

Tavraŋaquuq magitguq.
Qanuqtunuuq siniktiglaani nalugaa.

Tuġusuilaq.

II.

Maatnami—
Maani unniin nunami,

Mazaq uvva una uguŋainaaqtuq.
Qimugin pituilaq.

Ialiq aziŋatiqtuq.
Qugruit tiŋirut—

III.

Igiluu naniq,
Aŋaayaaġnazigaa.
Suli katumayaqłiuqtuŋa.

Saviġna.vaktut,
Ipkua siuliut
Qiniŋilaatiut.

IV.

Composition with Transformed Birds

Exiled from the cycle of star and stone,
The soil's fine extrusion of the final vein
Of blue shot through with gold,
Skull athrob with preoccupation.

In carving a song made manifest.
The receding field, our ensuing battle—
Though distant from home the ravens
More closely flock together.

The Orphan Girl

Of the three things she told me never to do,
     the first I am doing now.
The second I must have done,
     although I never meant injury.
The third I did and all too late.

Together then we fell asleep, lulled
     by the clamor of overpainted waves.

Nights likes these the wind insinuates
     in the interstitial rests when it doesn't
Come direct. By all means

Bereft, now following the widowbird,
     erratic, come near and far too soon.

Fugato (4)

At the house's entrance
Blood & its root of melting:
The bird means rain again.

The current's changed course,
Is moving upstream; turbulence
Arises from the void of the lake.

The bird's an eye extractor.
The bird devours vomit.

Claw of the moon, of iron & bone.

Rare Earth

Pans of ice where the land flattens
To the sea, to fracture and fissure
Of ice and water—

                were you to lay down
And die by not doing anything
To strengthen the weak,

The betrayal could fail,
Bone by bone. You would not be
Any smaller. You—

        no, you.

Nunaqtigiit

(people related through common possession of territory)

The enemy misled that missed the island in the fog,
I believe in one or the other, but both exist now
        to confuse me. Dark from dark.

Snow from snow. I believe in one—

Craggy boundary, knife blade at the throat's slight swell.

From time to time the sound of voices
                as through sun-singed grass,

or grasses that we used to insulate the walls of our winter houses—
walrus hides lashed together with rawhide cords.

So warm within the willows ingathered forced into leaf.

I am named for your sister Naviyuk: call me *apoŋ*.

Surely there are ghosts here, my children sprung
    from these deeper furrows.

The sky of my mind against which self-
                    betrayal in its sudden burn
    fails to describe the world.

We, who denied the landscape
           and saw the light of it.

Leaning against the stone wall ragged
I began to accept my past and, as I accepted it,

I felt, and I didn't understand:

I am bound to everyone.

Fugato (5)

Dead mouse the dead child
Once set in my hand,
Its gift a stiff slight heft.

With the bone of a bird,
The nail pulled loose
From weathered wood,

The house huddled
From rock on rock,
We are strong people.

Rete Mirabile

after Katexac

A large many-storied institution looming always,
        gabled trinity of windows jut from its thin skull.

Ribs of the skin boats, visible—not their double-seamed stitches,
        pulled taut without piercing through the walrus hides.

The men have retrieved a bowhead dead or killed it outright.
None of their faces ever fully legible.

It takes a pair to hoist the tail,
        another three grapple with a fin (pectoral).

    ★

The distinction between the ocean's blue & the whale's blue a matter of shades. The rocks that form the foundation of the undiminishable church echo the repetition of the rows of baleen in the whale's mouth.

    ★

Limb and fissure,
        plywood and driftwood, gouged withal—

Brayer to bone and back again.

*

The danger of breaking ice,
      the boat's keel.
Far off she had harvested the stalk
      long before its bloom.

*

On the strand between the buildings and the water's edge, a man
and woman. Perhaps a priest. Perhaps an elder. Perhaps a print-
maker. Perhaps one without allies. The man wears a collared shirt
in large plaid, trousers, and an eight-panel cap; his garments dif-
fer from the white hunting parka of a man in his prime. He is
carrying a bucket. The woman could be old or young. Her hair
is covered with a scarf folded triangularly; she wears an *atikluk*.
Both are walking away, upslope.

*

The lines are thick and distinct
           except when shapes and their suggestions

smudge with imprecision, incomplete
      either by chance of production or design.

*

The only human figure whose hands are empty is the woman, mid-stride. She is the wife of one of the hunters and the beloved (former?) of another. Of course this woman's hands hold no implements.

*

A pile of rock holds the land securely from the sea—
        a terminus, a vantage, a venture.

A rope twined below a prominent cliff. Here
        we   must sing   before we continue.

Innate

Cheek, tongue, headache—
I am a human being.

Daughter   *mother*
Asunder.

A shard of rock.
Now what was is no more.

Rivers, wind, salt—
A while ago,

I got hurt.
You are all unaware.

Mother   I forget.

Ilu

Uluaq, ukak, niaquŋ—
Inukguruŋa.

Panik   *aakaa*
Avvak.

Uyaġauramik.
Maatnami imma pitaiqutuq.

Kurgit, nuġi, tagiuq—
Akkuni,

Atniqtuŋa.
Nalurusi.

Aakaa   puuyanatuŋa.

Ugiuvak/King Island

A line of white birds ends in nothing.
The falling song of women unseen
Twists between rock spires,
Our distant island
Haunted by the numberless.

From the deep shade of the gully
The water continues to rise.

Unbound from the slum
That backs to black bogs
Surrounded by gravel,

Take us back.

ACKNOWLEDGMENTS

Grateful acknowledgment is made to the editors of the following publications in which versions of these poems have appeared:

Apogee: "Akkumin Qantiq/Swift Descent" and "Composition with Transformed Birds"; *Colorado Review*: "Rete Mirabile"; *Drunken Boat*: "In a House Apart," "Mother Tongues," "Etch," and "Ugiuvak/King Island"; *Ice Floe*: "Ilu/Innate," "The Dissolve of Voices," and "Maliktuq/Procession"; *Poetry Northeast*: "Ivory, Stomach, Bone," "At Anaktuvuk Pass," "Fugato," and "Love Poem"; *Prairie Schooner*: "Force Majeur," "Mysteries of Light," "Disappearer," "Muġnatuŋilaŋa/I am not tired," "On Either Side," "Time and Time Again," and "Looking Through"; *Sing: Poetry of the Indigenous Americas*: "Hyperboreal" and "Intervale"; *Talking Stick Quarterly*: "Drawn Together"; *YARN*: "In Long Light"